Coach

Coach

365 DAYS
OF
INSPIRATION
for Coaches and Players

With an Introduction By
MATTHEW KELLY

BLUE SPARROW
North Palm Beach, Florida

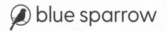

blue sparrow

Copyright © 2020
Kakadu, LLC
Published by Blue Sparrow

The quotes in this book have been drawn from dozens
of sources. They are assumed to be accurate as quoted in
their previously published forms. Although every effort
has been made to verify the quotes and sources, the
Publisher cannot guarantee their perfect accuracy.

Design by Ashley Wirfel and Madeline Harris

ISBN: 978-1-63582-149-9 (hardcover)
ISBN: 978-1-63582-148-2 (e-Book)

10   9   8   7   6   5   4   3   2   1

Printed in the United States of America

FIRST EDITION

Table of Contents

INTRODUCTION
1

JANUARY
5

FEBRUARY
37

MARCH
67

APRIL
99

MAY
131

JUNE
163

JULY
195

AUGUST
227

SEPTEMBER
259

OCTOBER
291

NOVEMBER
323

DECEMBER
355

Introduction

───────────

YOU ARE A COACH. Whether you're aware of it or not, you are a coach. How do I know? Because everyone is a coach. You may not wear a uniform and give signals from third base. You may not draft up plays and give post-game interviews. You may not even follow sports. **But you are a coach.**

Everyone is a coach.

And everyone *needs* coaching. There are people in your life who need *you* to coach them—to strive for better and to become more. And there are people in your life whom you need to coach *you*—to strive for better and to become more. In fact, the best of the best—the Hall of Famers and Olympians and Legends—all have two things in common, no matter the sport or the era:

1. They all had great coaches.
2. They all loved to be coached.

Because behind every great athlete is a string of great coaches. They come into our lives at different times for different reasons. Sometimes, they come into your life to change your life or perspective completely. And sometimes they come into your life to teach you just one lesson, but maybe that one lesson is exactly what you needed to reach the next level.

Behind every hard-fought yard, you'll find a coach demanding more. Behind every game-winning play, you'll find a coach asking for better. Behind every grueling stride toward the finish line, you'll find a coach pushing, sweating, encouraging. Behind every difficult life decision made—and made well—you'll find a coach who knows what reaching your true potential looks like.

You are a coach. I am a coach. Everyone is a coach. And as coaches, it is our duty to draw the best out of the people we love, to help them become the-best-version-of-themselves.

Perhaps no one has expressed this sentiment better than Shannon Sharpe, one of the best Tight Ends in the history of the NFL. In the summer of 2009, Sharpe gave an emotional speech for his Hall of Fame induction. The speech was about 26 minutes long. He didn't thank his agent. He didn't thank his high school or college coaches. He didn't even thank Denver Bronco's head coach Mike Shanahan. Who did he thank? His grandma—the woman who raised him:

"My grandmother didn't teach me how to throw a ball. She didn't teach me how to catch a ball. She didn't teach me technique, how to run fast. She didn't teach me anything about sports. She taught me how to be a man."

How to live, how to be, how to *become*—more, greater, better. This is at the heart of what it means to be a coach. No coach settles for a-second-rate-version of his players. The most effective coaches demand the best *from* their players, and they desire the best *for* their players.

An adequate coach teaches. A good coach leads. A great coach inspires. **The best coaches love.**

You are a coach. What kind of coach will you be?

January

January 1

"Leaders are made, they are not born. They are made by hard effort which is the price which all of us must pay to achieve any goal that is worthwhile."

Vince Lombardi
NFL Head Coach

January 2

"If you fail to prepare, you're prepared to fail."

Mark Spitz
Olympic Swimmer

January 3

"I've missed more than nine thousand shots in my career. I've lost almost three hundred games. Twenty-six times, I've been trusted to take the game winning shot and missed. I've failed over and over and over again in my life. And that is why I succeed."

Michael Jordan
NBA Player

January 4

"Talent sets the floor, character sets the ceiling."

Bill Belichick
NFL Head Coach

January 5

"Success is where preparation and opportunity meet."

Bobby Unser
Professional Racecar Driver

January 6

"In baseball and in business, there are three types of people. Those who make it happen, those who watch it happen, and those who wonder what happened."

Tommy Lasorda
MLB Manager

January 7

"Today, do what others won't so tomorrow you can accomplish what others can't."

Simone Biles
U.S. Olympic Gymnast

January 8

"All the physical comes from the mental."

Clara Hughes
Canadain Olympic Cyclist

January 9

"Every leader needs to remember that a healthy respect for authority takes time to develop. It's like building trust. You don't instantly have trust, it has to be earned."

Mike Krzyzewski
College Basketball Head Coach

January 10

"You are never really playing an opponent.
You are playing yourself, your own highest
standards, and when you reach your limits,
that is real joy."

Arthur Ashe
Tennis Player

January 11

"No one achieves excellence at anything without coaching."

Matthew Kelly
Author

January 12

"Hard work beats talent when talent doesn't work hard."

Tim Notke
High School Basketball Coach

January 13

"The strength of the team is each individual member. The strength of each member is the team."

Phil Jackson
NBA Head Coach

January 14

"The most powerful leadership tool you have is your own personal example."

John Wooden
College Basketball Head Coach

January 15

"Nobody who ever gave his best, regretted it."

George S. Halas
NFL Head Coach

January 16

"The measure of who we are is how we react
to something that doesn't go our way."

Gregg Popovich
NBA Head Coach

January 17

"Without self-discipline, success is impossible, period."

Lou Holtz
College Football Head Coach

January 18

"You can't put a limit on anything. The more
you dream, the farther you get."

Michael Phelps
U.S. Olympic Swimmer

January 19

"Coaching is 90% attitude and 10% technique."

Author Unknown

January 20

"Strength does not come from winning. Your struggles develop your strengths."

Arnold Schwarzenegger
Governor of California

January 21

"In leadership, there are no words more important than trust. In any organization, trust must be developed among every member of the team if success is going to be achieved."

Mike Krzyzewski
College Basketball Head Coach

January 22

"If you can't outplay them, outwork them."

Ben Hogan
Professional Golfer

January 23

"There are only two options regarding commitment. You're either IN or you're OUT. There is no such thing as life in-between."

Pat Riley
NBA Head Coach

January 24

"Obstacles don't have to stop you. If you run into a wall, don't turn around and give up. Figure out how to climb it, go through it, or work around it."

Michael Jordan
NBA Player

January 25

"Never give up! Failure and rejection are only the first step to succeeding."

Jim Valvano
College Basketball Head Coach

January 26

"First master the fundamentals."

Larry Bird
NBA Player

January 27

"There are two pains in life. There is the pain of discipline and the pain of disappointment. If you can handle the pain of discipline, then you'll never have to deal with the pain of disappointment."

Nick Saban
College Football Head Coach

January 28

"To live in the past is to die in the present."

Bill Belichick
NFL Head Coach

January 29

"Winning isn't everything, but wanting to win is."

Vince Lombardi
NFL Head Coach

January 30

"To uncover your true potential you must first find your own limits and then you have to have the courage to blow past them."

Picabo Street
U.S. Olympic Skier

January 31

"You can't always control circumstances—you can always control your attitude, approach, and response."

Tony Dungy
NFL Coach

February 1

"A champion is someone who gets up when he can't."

Jack Dempsey
Professional

February 2

"As coaches, we equip people to be in touch
with their best selves."

Clyde Lowstuter
35 Truths: Lessons from
the Front Lines of Executive Coaching

February 3

"Always make a total effort, even when the odds are against you."

Arnold Palmer
Professional Golfer

February 4

"You miss 100% of the shots you don't take."

Wayne Gretzky
NHL Player

February 5

"The only person who can stop you from reaching your goals is you."

Jackie Joyner-Kersee
U.S. Olympic Track and Field

February 6

"Make sure that team members know they
are working with you, not for you."

John Wooden
College Basketball Head Coach

February 7

"If you want to win, do the ordinary things better than anyone else does them day in and day out."

Chuck Noll
NFL Head Coach

February 8

"Stay focused, your start does not determine how you're going to finish."

Herm Edwards
NFL Head Coach

February 9

"Success isn't measured by money or power or social rank. Success is measured by your discipline and inner peace."

Mike Ditka
NFL Head Coach

February 10

"If it is easy then you're doing it wrong."

Gabby Williams
Professional Basketball Player

February 11

"I've observed that if individuals who prevail in a high competitive environment have any one thing in common besides success, it is failure—and their ability to overcome it."

Bill Walsh
NFL Head Coach

February 12

"Never let the fear of striking out get in your
way."

Babe Ruth
MLB Player

February 13

"The only correct actions are those that demand no explanation and no apology."

Red Auerbach
NBA Head Coach

February 14

"Ability is what you're capable of doing. Motivation determines what you do. Attitude determines how well you do it."

Lou Holtz
College Football Head Coach

February 15

"If you don't love what you do, you won't do it with much conviction or passion."

Mia Hamm
U.S. Olympic Soccer Player

February 16

"It's different as a coach because you feel responsible for a lot of people. Even though you don't take a shot, you don't get a rebound, you feel like you just want people to succeed and you want to help them any way you can."

Steve Kerr
NBA Head Coach

February 17

"It's hard to beat a person who never gives up."

Babe Ruth
MLB Player

February 18

"You have to expect things of yourself before you can do them."

Michael Jordan
NBA Player

February 19

"Impossible is just a big word thrown around by small men who find it easier to live in the world they've been given than to explore the power they have to change it. Impossible is not a fact. It's an opinion. Impossible is not a declaration. It's a dare. Impossible is potential. Impossible is temporary. Impossible is nothing."

Muhammed Ali
Professional Boxer

February 20

"Coaches have to watch for what they don't want to see and listen to what they don't want to hear."

John Madden
NFL Head Coach

February 21

"It's not just about working hard, it's about working together. You have to care more about the team than you do about yourself."

John Calipari
College Basketball Head Coach

February 22

"To give any less than your best is to sacrifice a gift."

Steve Prefontaine
U.S. Olympic Runner

February 23

"Champions keep playing until they get it right."

Billie Jean King
Professional Tennis Player

February 24

"During critical periods, a leader is not allowed to feel sorry for himself, to be down, to be angry, or to be weak. Leaders must beat back these emotions."

Mike Krzyzewski
College Basketball Head Coach

February 25

"The most important thing is to try and inspire people so that they can be great at whatever they want to do."

Kobe Bryant
NBA Player

February 26

"Courage doesn't mean you get afraid.
Courage means you don't let fear stop you."

Bethany Hamilton
Professional Surfer

February 27

"An athlete cannot run with money in his pockets. He must run with hope in his heart and dreams in his head."

Emil Zatopek
Professional Runner

February 28

"The difference between ordinary and
extraordinary is that little extra."

Jimmy Johnson
NFL Head Coach

February 29

"When you're in the day to day grind, it just seems like it's another step along the way. But I find joy in the actual process, the journey, the work. It's not the end. It's not the end event."

Cal Ripken Jr.
MLB Player

March

March 1

"Coaches are aware of how to ignite passion and motivate people. They have an energy that is contagious and know exactly how to get their team excited."

Brian Cagneey
Author, Coaching

March 2

"We are all capable of doing one thing better than any other person alive at this time in history."

Matthew Kelly
New York Times Bestselling Author

March 3

"Life is 10% what happens to you and 90% how you respond to it."

Lou Holtz
College Football Head Coach

March 4

"I think that the good and the great are only separated by the willingness to sacrifice."

Kareem Abdul-Jabar
NBA Player

March 5

"The principle is competing against yourself. It's about self-improvement, about being better than you were the day before."

Steve Young
NFL Player

March 6

"Seek opportunities to show you care. The smallest gestures often make the biggest difference."

John Wooden
College Basketball Head Coach

March 7

"Acknowledge your small victories. They will eventually add up to something great."

Kara Goucher
U.S Olympic Runner

March 8

"That's why at the start of every season I always encouraged players to focus on the journey rather than the goal. What matters most is playing the game the right way and having the courage to grow, as human beings as well as basketball players. When you do that, the ring takes care of itself."

Phil Jackson
NBA Head Coach

March 9

"If you have everything under control, you're not moving fast enough."

Mario Andretti
Professional Racecar Driver

March 10

"During my 18 years I came to bat almost 10,000 times. I struck out about 1,700 times and walked maybe 1,800 times. You can figure a ballplayer will average about 500 at bats a season. That means I played seven years without ever hitting the ball."

Mickey Mantle
MLB Player

March 11

"An acre of performance is worth a whole world of promise."

Red Auerbach
NBA Head Coach

March 12

"The best coaches know what the end result looks like, whether it's an offensive play, a defensive play, a defensive coverage, or just some idea of the organization."

Vince Lombardi
NFL Head Coach

March 13

"People will exceed targets they set themselves."

Gordon Dryden, Author
The Learning Revolution

March 14

"It isn't the mountain ahead to climb that wears you out, it's the pebble in your shoe."

Mohammad Ali
Professional Boxer

March 15

"Age is no barrier. It's a limitation you put on your mind."

Jackie Joyner-Kersee
U.S. Olympic Track and Field

March 16

"I realized that life had much more to offer than I had anticipated and decided to help others in their human journey. Thus, I become a trainer and a coach with passion for transformation."

Ann Betz
Coaching the Spirit

March 17

"I want my team to be more detached from the wins and losses and be more focused on doing the little things well. When you focus on getting the win, it can suffocate you, especially during the playoffs when the pressure gets thick."

Sue Enquist
College Softball Coach

March 20

"A trophy carries dust. Memories last forever."

Mary Lou Retton
U.S. Olympic Gymnast

March 19

"There may be people that have more talent than you, but there's no excuse for anyone to work harder than you do."

Derek Jeter
MLB Player

March 20

"Persistence can change failure into
extraordinary achievement."

Attributed to Multiple People

March 21

"Set your goals high, and don't stop till you get there."

Bo Jackson
NBA and NFL Player

March 22

"I never learn anything talking. I only learn
things when I ask questions."

Steve Prefontaine
U.S. Olympic Runner

March 23

"Winning and championships are memorable, but they come from the strength of the relationships."

Jim Calhoun
College Basketball Head Coach

March 24

"Never give up, Never give in, and when the upper hand is ours, may we have the ability to handle the win with dignity."

Doug Williams
NFL Coach

March 25

"The most valuable player is the one who makes the most players valuable."

Payton Manning
NFL Player

March 26

"Most people never run far enough on their first wind to find out they've got a second."

William James, Psychologist
Philosopher, Author

March 27

"My responsibility is leadership, and the minute I get negative, that is going to have an influence on my team."

Don Shula
NFL Head Coach

March 28

"You don't win with X's and O's. What you win with is people."

Joe Gibbs
NFL Head Coach

March 29

"Good is not good when better is expected."

Vin Scully
MLB Broadcaster

March 30

"Leadership, like coaching, is fighting for the hearts and souls of men and getting them to believe in you."

Eddie Robinson
NFL Coach

March 31

"You were born to be a player. You were meant to be here. This moment is yours."

Herb Brooks
U.S. Olympic Hockey Coach

April 1

"A coach is someone who can give correction without causing resentment."

John Wooden
College Basketball Head Coach

April 2

"The more difficult the victory, the greater
the happiness in winning."

Pelé
Brazzillain Professional Soccer Player

April 3

"One man can be a crucial ingredient on a team, but one man cannot make a team."

Kareem Abdul-Jabbar
NBA Player

April 4

"You can motivate by fear, and you can motivate by reward. But both those methods are only temporary. The only lasting thing is self-motivation."

Homer Rice
College Football Head Coach

April 5

"Don't be afraid if things seem difficult in the beginning. That's only the initial impression. The important thing is not to retreat: you have to master yourself."

Olga Korbut
Russian Olympic Gymnast

April 6

"Our emphasis is on execution, not winning."

Pat Summitt
College Basketball Head Coach

April 7

"He who is not courageous enough to take risks will accomplish nothing in life."

Muhammed Ali
Professional Boxer

April 8

"I need people who look at adversity as a challenge and failure as a learning opportunity."

John Calipari
College Basketball Head Coach

April 9

"Approach the game with no preset agendas and you'll probably come away surprised at your overall efforts."

Phil Jackson
NBA Head Coach

April 10

"I didn't believe in team motivation. I believe in getting a team prepared so it knows it will have the necessary confidence when it steps on the field and be prepared to play a good game."

Tom Landry
NFL Player

April 11

"Never let your head hang down. Never give up and sit down and grieve. Find another way."

Satchel Paige
MLB Player

"They say discipline and dedication and respect are the key factors, but patience is a virtue that is absolutely essential!"

Ria Ramnarine
Professional Boxer

April 13

"In the beginning we form our habits, after awhile they begin to form us. If we do not conquer our bad habits, sooner or later they conquer us."

Matthew Kelly

April 14

"Do you know what my favorite part of the game is? The opportunity to play."

Mike Singletary,
NFL Head Coach

April 15

"It is not the size of a man but the size of his heart that matters."

Evander Holyfield
Professional Boxer

April 16

"Wisdom is always an overmatch for strength."

Phil Jackson
NBA Head Coach

April 17

"It's not whether you get knocked down; it's whether you get up."

Vince Lombardi
NFL Head Coach

April 18

"A good coach will make his players see what they can be rather than what they are."

Ara Parasheghian
College Football Head Coach

April 19

"Never say never because limits, like fears, are often just an illusion."

Michael Jordan
NBA Player

April 20

"It's not the will to win that matters—everyone has that. It's the will to prepare to win that matters."

Paul "Bear" Bryant
College Football Head Coach

April 21

"What makes something special is not just what you have to gain, but what you feel there is to lose."

Andre Agassi
U.S. Olympic Tennis Player

"If you sit back and spend too much time feeling good about what you did in the past, you're going to come up short next time."

Bill Belichick
NFL Head Coach

April 23

"One man practicing sportsmanship is far better than a hundred teaching it."

Knute Rockne
College Football Head Coach

April 24

"I've learned that something constructive
comes from every defeat."

Tom Landry
NFL Head Coach

April 25

"Excellence is the gradual result of always striving to do better."

Pat Riley
NBA Head Coach

April 26

"Just keep going. Everybody gets better if they keep at it."

Ted Williams
MLB Player

April 27

"What to do with a mistake: recognize it, admit it, learn from it, forget it."

Dean Smith
College Basketball Head Coach

"Gold medals aren't really made of gold. They're made of sweat, determination, and a hard-to-find alloy called guts."

Dan Gable
U.S. Olympic Wrestler

April 29

"Don't ever let your memories be bigger than your dreams."

Jim Craig
U.S. Olympic Hockey Player

April 30

"We can push ourselves further. We always
have more to give."

Simone Biles
U.S. Olympic Gymnast

May 1

"Winners never quit and quitters never win."

Vince Lombardi
NFL Head Coach

May 2

"If you aren't going all the way, why go at all?"

Joe Namath
NFL Player

May 3

"Pain is temporary. It may last a minute, or an hour, or a day, or a year, but eventually it will subside and something else will take its place. If I quit, however, it lasts forever."

Lance Armstrong
Professional Cyclist

May 4

"Be more concerned with your character than your reputation. Because your character is what you really are, while your reputation is merely what others think you are."

John Wooden
College Basketball Head Coach

May 5

"You're never a loser until you quit trying."

Mike Ditka
NFL Head Coach

"How you respond to the challenge in the second half will determine what you become after the game, whether you are a winner or a loser."

Lou Holtz
College Football Head Coach

May 7

"What type of teammates do you want to play with? Be that teammate yourself."

John Calipari
College Basketball Head Coach

May 8

"Only a man who knows what it is like to be defeated can reach down to the bottom of his soul and come up with the extra ounce of power it takes to win when the match is even."

Muhammed Ali
Professional Boxer

May 9

"You must be prepared to dare to be
different in a world where uniformatity is safe
and rewarded."

Matthew Kelly
Author

May 10

"Push yourself again and again. Don't give an inch until the final buzzer sounds."

Larry Bird
NBA Player

May 11

"I don't think about the miles that are coming down the road, I don't think about the mile I'm on right now, I don't think about the miles I've already covered. I think about what I'm doing right now, just being lost in the moment."

Ryan Hall
MMA Instructor

May 12

"You get better when your best effort
becomes your way of life."

Tom Crean
College Basketball Head Coach

May 13

"The definition of courage is going from defeat to defeat with enthusiasm."

Winston Churchill
Former British Prime Minister

"If you're going to have a team of role players, then you better have a team of players who truly understand their roles."

Steve Kerr
NBA Head Coach

May 15

"I think the most important thing about coaching is that you have to have a sense of confidence about what you're doing. You have to be a salesman and you have to get your players, particularly your leaders, to believe in what you're trying to accomplish on the basketball floor."

Phil Jackson
NBA Head Coach

May 16

"Are you going to stand or are you going to crumble? In the face of everything, stand still."

Gabby Douglas
U.S. Olympic Gymnast

May 17

"Every choice, every decision, everything we do everyday, we want to be a champion."

Nick Saban
College Football Head Coach

May 18

"Football doesn't build character, it reveals character."

Marv Levy
NFL Head Coach

May 19

"I've never felt my job was to win basketball games—rather, that the essence of my job as a coach was to do everything I could to give my players the background necessary to succeed in life."

Bobby Knight
College Basketball Head Coach

May 20

"Never quit. It is the easiest cop-out in the world. Set a goal and don't quit until you attain it. When you do attain it, set another goal, and don't quit until you reach it. Never quit."

Paul "Bear" Bryant
College Football Head Coach

May 21

"Perfection is not attainable. But if we chase perfection, we can catch excellence."

Vince Lombardi
NFL Head Coach

May 22

"Don't count the days; make the days count."

Muhammed Ali
Professional Boxer

May 23

"Winning doesn't always mean being first. Winning means you're doing better than you've ever done before."

Bonnie Blair
US Olympic Speed Skater

May 24

"Some people want it to happen, some wish it would happen, others make it happen."

Michael Jordan
NBA Player

May 25

"Do not let what you can't do interfere with what you can do."

John Wooden
College Basketball Head Coach

May 26

"Leadership is a matter of having people look at you and gain confidence . . . If you're in control, they're in control."

Tom Landry
NFL Head Coach

May 27

"If you don't have confidence, you'll always find a way not to win."

Carl Lewis
Olympic Track and Field Gold Medalist

May 28

"What keeps me going is not winning, but the quest for reaching potential in myself as a coach and my kids as divers. It's the pursuit of excellence."

Ron O Brien
Olympic Diving Coach

May 29

"If everyone in my locker room is bright, smart, motivated and a team player, we have a chance to beat anyone that we play."

David Shaw
Head Football Coach

May 30

"Adversity causes some men to break; others to break records."

William A Ward
Inspirational Writer

May 31

"If everyone in my locker room is bright, smart, motivated and a team player, we have a chance to beat anyone that we play."

David Shaw
Head Football Coach

June

June 1

"Who you become is infinitely more important than what you do or what you have."

Matthew Kelly
Author

"The first thing is to love your sport. Never do it to please someone else. It has to be yours."

Peggy Fleming
US Olympic Figure Skater

June 3

"The hardest skill to acquire in this sport is the one where you compete all out, give it all you have, and you are still getting beat no matter what you do. When you have the killer instinct to fight through that, it is very special."

Eddie Reese
Olympic Swim Coach

June 4

"Failure is good. It's fertilizer. Everything I've learned about coaching, I've learned from making mistakes."

Rick Pitino
College Basketball Head Coach

June 5

"To have long term success as a coach or in any position of leadership, you have to be obsessed in some way."

Pat Riley
NBA Head Coach

June 6

"Good teams become great ones when
the members trust each other enough to
surrender the me for the we."

Phil Jackson
NBA Head Coach

June 7

"Don't worry about losing. Think about winning."

Mike Kryzyzewski
College Basketball Head Coach

June 8

"We have opportunities all around us—
sometimes we just don't recognize them."

Lou Holtz
College Football Head Coach

June 9

"Winning is the science of being totally prepared."

George Allen
NFL Coach

June 10

"Concentration is a fine antidote to anxiety."

Jack Nicklaus
Professional Golfer

June 11

"Really, coaching is simplicity. It's getting players to play better than they think that they can."

Tom Landry
NFL Head Coach

June 12

"Never put an age limit on your dreams."

Dara Torres
U.S. Olympic Swimmer

June 13

"A life is not important except in the impact it has on other lives."

Jackie Robinson
MLB Player

June 14

"If anything goes bad, I did it. If anything goes semi-good, we did it. If anything goes really good, then you did it. That's all it takes to get people to win football games for you."

Paul "Bear" Bryant
College Football Head Coach

June 15

"Success isn't owned, it's leased. And, rent is due every day."

J.J. Watt
NFL PLayer

June 16

"The more that you seek the uncomfortable,
the more you will become comfortable."

Connor McGregor
Professional Mixed Martial Artist

June 17

"Make time for it. Just get it done. Nobody ever got strong or got in shape by thinking about it. They did it."

Arnold Schwarzenegger
Governor of California

June 18

"There are better starters than me, but I'm a stronger finisher."

Usain Bolt
Jamaican Olympic Sprinter

June 19

"Champions aren't made in gyms.
Champions are made from something that
they have deep inside them—a desire, a
dream, a vision."

Muhammad Ali
Professional Boxer

June 20

"You win a few, you lose a few. Some get rained out. But you got to dress for all of them."

Satchel Paige
MLB PLayer

June 21

"It doesn't matter what your background is or where you come from. If you have dreams and goals, that's all that matters."

Serena Williams
Professional Tennis Player

June 22

"Great football coaches have the vision to see, the faith to believe, the courage to do—and 25 great players."

Marv Levy
NFL Head Coach

June 23

"Basketball is a pretty simple game. What wins is consistency and competitiveness."

Gregg Popovich
NBA Head Coach

June 24

"The most luxurious possession, the richest treasure anybody has, is his personal dignity."

Jackie Robinson
MLB Player

June 25

"The secret of winning is working more as a team and less as individuals."

Knute Rockne
College Football Head Coach

June 26

"Think about your dream. Then, put your head down and go to work."

Dabo Swinney
College Football Head Coach

June 27

"Confidence is the most important single factor in this game, and no matter how great your natural talent, there is only one way to obtain and sustain it: work."

Jack Nicklaus
Professional Golfer

June 28

"True champions aren't always the ones that win, but those with the most guts."

Mia Hamm
U.S. Olympic Soccer Player

June 29

"It doesn't matter what you're trying to accomplish. It's all a matter of discipline."

Wilma Rudolph
U.S. Olympic Runner

June 30

"Concentration blocks out pressure. If you make mistakes and look for excuses, you lose your concentration and feel pressure. I try to keep from doing that."

Jack Nicklaus
Professional Golfer

July

July 1

"Show me someone who has done something worthwhile, and I'll show you someone who has overcome adversity."

Lou Holtz
College Football Head Coach

July 2

"Good, better, best. Never let it rest. Until your good is better and your better is best."

Tim Duncan
NBA Player

July 3

"Failure isn't fatal. But, failure to change might be."

John Wooden
College Basketball Head Coach

July 4

"Set realistic goals, keep re-evaluating, and be consistent."

Venus Williams
Profession Tennis Player

July 5

"You don't demand respect, you earn it."

Steve Seidler
Assistant College Basketball Coach

July 6

"All coaching is, is taking a player where he can't take himself."

Bill McCartney
College Football Head Coach

July 7

"Rather than focusing on the obstacle in your path, focus on the bridge over the obstacle."

Mary Lou Retton
U.S. Olympic Gymnast

July 8

"We all have dreams. But in order to make dreams come into reality, it takes an awful lot of determination, dedication, self-discipline, and effort."

Jesse Owens
U.S. Olympic Track and Field

July 9

"I can accept failure, everyone fails at something. But I can't accept not trying."

Michael Jordan
NBA Player

July 10

"Not to get too clever, but "consistent effort
is a consistent challenge."

Bill Walsh
NFL Head Coach

July 11

"Pain doesn't tell you when you ought to stop. Pain is the little voice in your head that tries to hold you back because it knows if you continue you will change."

Kobe Bryant
NBA Player

July 12

"It is a fine thing to have ability, but the ability to discover ability in others is the true test."

Lou Holtz
College Football Head Coach

July 13

"There is a popular fallacy that falling down is the mark of a poor skater. But the truth is that when one stops falling, he has probably stopped improving."

Dick Button
US Olympic Figure Skater

"We have to fight the entire time, we can't start at the end when it's getting down to crunch time. We can't leave anything on the floor."

Kerri Walsh
U.S. Olympic Volleyball Player

July 15

"The hard days are the best because that's where champions are made."

Gabby Douglas
U.S. Olympic Gymnast

July 16

"Run when you can, walk when you have to,
crawl if you must; just never give up."

Dean Karnazes
American Ultramarathon Runner

July 17

"Always work hard, never give up, and fight until the end because it's never really over until the whistle blows."

Alex Morgan
U.S. Olympic Soccer Player

July 18

"Take those chances and you can achieve greatness, whereas if you go conservative, you'll never know. I truly believe what doesn't kill you makes you stronger. Even if you fail, learning and moving on is sometimes the best thing."

Danica Patrick
Professional Racecar Drive

July 19

"Success is peace of mind which is a direct result of self-satisfaction in knowing you did your best to become the best you are capable of becoming."

John Wooden
College Basketball Head Coach

July 20

"You should never stay at the same level.
Always push yourself to the next."

Marnelli Dimzon
Head Coach Philippines Women's
National Football Team

July 21

"Leadership is more about responsibility than ability!"

Jim Tunney
NFL Official

"Far more coaches fail to achieve success because they lack ability to develop team culture rather than because they lack good direction or knowledge of the game."

Unknown Author

July 23

"To have any doubt in your body is the biggest weakness an athlete can have."

Shawn Johnson
U.S. Olympic Gymnast

July 24

"Once you know what failure feels like,
determination chases success."

Kobe Bryant
NBA Player

July 25

"No matter what the competition is, I try to find a goal that day and better that goal."

Bonnie Blair
U.S. Olympic Speed Skater

"If you're unwilling to leave someplace you've outgrown, you will never reach your full potential. To be the best, you have to constantly be challenging yourself, raising the bar, pushing the limits of what you can do. Don't stand still, leap forward."

Ronda Rousey
Professional Mixed Martial Artist

July 27

"Each of us has a fire in our hearts for something, it's our goal in life to find it and keep it."

Mary Lou Retton
U.S. Olympic Gymnast

July 28

"Take your victories, whatever they may be, cherish them, use them, but don't settle for them."

Mia Hamm
U.S. Olympic Soccer Player

July 29

"A strong mind is one of the key components that separates the great from the good."

Gary Player
Professional Golfer

July 30

"A champion needs motivation above and beyond winning."

Pat Riley
NBA Head Coach

July 31

"The only one who can tell you "you can't win" is you and you don't have to listen."

Jessica Ennis
British Olympic Track and Field Athlete

August 1

"Don't practice till you get it right, practice till you can't get it wrong."

McKayla Maroney
US Olympic Gymnast

August 2

"Success isn't always about greatness, it's about consistency. Consistent, hard work gains success. The rest will come."

Dwayne "The Rock" Johnson
Actor

August 3

"The interesting thing about coaching is that you have to trouble the comfortable, and comfort the troubled."

Ric Charlesworth
Australian Sports Coach

August 4

"If you're bored with life - you don't get up every morning with a burning desire to do things - you don't have enough goals."

Lou Holtz
College Football Head Coach

August 5

"A coach should never be afraid to ask questions of anyone he could learn from."

Bobby Knight
College Basketball Head Coach

August 6

"If things don't come easy, there is no premium on effort. There should be joy in the chase, zest in the pursuit."

Branch Rickey
MLB Player

August 7

"I have a rule on my team: When we talk to one another, we look each other right in the eye, because I think it's tough to lie to somebody. You give respect to somebody."

Mike Krzyzewski
College Basketball Head Coach

August 8

"Be the best version of yourself: for yourself,
your team mates, and everyone you're
representing."

Katie Richardson-Walsh
British Olympic Field Hockey Player

August 9

"The only place that success comes before work is in the dictionary."

Vince Lombardi
NFL Head Coach

August 10

"So much can be accomplished in one moment of courage. And so much can be lost to one moment of fear."

Matthew Kelly
Author

August 11

"We have the can-do factor, and us doing what we do I think inspires people to just try that little bit harder, whether they are able—bodied or disabled."

Lee Pearson
British Paralympic Equestrian

August 12

"Keep working, even when no one is watching."

Alex Morgan
U.S. Olympic Soccer Player

August 13

"Believe me, the reward is not so great without the struggle."

Wilma Rudolph
U.S. Olympic Runner

August 14

"The more I have been involved in Football, the more I realize that individual talent is minimized or maximized by the environment those blokes go into."

Leigh Matthews
Australian Football League

August 15

"Talent wins games, but teamwork and intelligence wins championships."

Michael Jordan
NBA Player

August 16

"You've got to be confident when you're competing. You've got to be a beast."

Gabby Douglas
U.S. Olympic Gymnast

August 17

"Success is that place in the road where preparation meets opportunity."

Branch Rickey
MLB Player

August 18

"The most important thing in the Olympic Games is not winning but taking part; the essential thing in life is not conquering but fighting well."

Pierre de Coubertin
Father of the Modern Olympic Games

August 19

"Passion first and everything will fall into place."

Holly Holm
Professional Mixed Martial Artist

August 20

"Once you give them the power to tell you you're great, you've also given them the power to tell you you're unworthy. Once you start caring about people's opinions of you, you give up control."

Ronda Rousey
Professional Mixed Martial Artist

August 21

"Never surrender opportunity to security."

Branch Rickey
MLB Player

August 22

"If you can't go through it, find a way around it.
Don't spend all your time banging your head."

Lenny Wilkens
NBA Player

August 23

"Focus on remedies, not faults."

Jack Nicklaus
American Professional Golfer

August 24

"To have harmony on a team, you need a coach who can get inside the head of every player and get them all pulling in one direction."

Jerry West
NBA Player

August 25

"A defining characteristic of a good leader is the conviction that he or she can make a positive difference—can prevail even when the odds are stacked against him or her. A successful leader is not easily swayed from this self-belief. But it happens."

Bill Walsh
NFL Head Coach

August 26

"I think the real free person in society is one that's disciplined. It's the one that can choose; that is the free one."

Dean Smith
College Basketball Head Coach

August 27

"The man who has no imagination has no wings."

Muhammad Ali
Professional Boxer

August 28

"When you win, say nothing. When you lose,
say less."

Paul Brown
NFL Head Coach

August 29

"The only way to prove that you're a good sport is to lose."

Ernie Banks
MLB Player

August 30

"Erase the word "failure" from your vocabulary. No case is ever truly closed, and no challenge is ever over."

Mary Lou Retton
U.S. Olympic Gymnast

August 31

"I don't plan on being disappointed. We plan on being really good, and obviously, we plan on winning."

Gregg Troy
College Swimming Head Coach

September

September 1

"A good coach can change a game. A great coach can change a life."

John Wooden
College Basketball Head Coach

September 2

"I won't accept anything less than the best a player's capable of doing . . . and he has the right to expect the best that I can do for him and the team!"

Lou Holtz
College Football Head Coach

September 3

"Anything is always a possibility. Wouldn't talk about what we would have done or what we would do. Everything is a possibility."

Jim Harbaugh
College Football Head Coach

September 4

"A coach is someone who tells you what you don't want to hear, who has you see what you don't want to see, so you can be who you have always known you could be."

Tom Landry
NFL Head Coach

September 5

"Don't look back. Something might be gaining on you."

Satchel Paige
MLB Player

"This ability to conquer oneself is no doubt
the most precious of all things sports
bestows."

Olga Korbuit
Soviet Union Olympic Gymnast

September 7

"If they think your dreams are crazy, show them what crazy dreams can do."

Serena Williams
Professional Tennis Player

September 8

"The greatest asset is a strong mind. If I know someone is training harder than I am, I have no excuses."

P.V. Sindhu
Indian Professional Badminton Player

September 9

"If you have something critical to say to a player, preface it by saying something positive. That way when you get to the criticism, at least you know he'll be listening."

Bud Grant
NFL Head Coach

September 10

"Everything negative—pressure, challenges—
is all an opportunity for me to rise."

Kobe Bryant
NBA Player

September 11

"It's not about winning at the Olympic Games. It's about trying to win. The motto is faster, higher, stronger, not fastest, highest, strongest. Sometimes it's the trying that matters."

Bronte Barratt
Australian Olympic Swimmer

September 12

"Don't be a spectator, don't let life pass you by."

Lou Holtz
College Football Head Coach

September 13

"When you fall, get right back up. Just keep going, keep pushing it."

Lindsey Vonn
U.S. Olympic Skier

September 14

"It's the one thing you can control. You are responsible for how people remember you— or don't. So don't take it lightly."

Kobe Bryant
NBA Player

September 15

"As much time as you put into it, that's what your achievements are going to be when you come out of it."

Mary Lou Retton
U.S. Olympic Gymnast

September 16

"There are always new, grander challenges
to confront, and a true winner will embrace
each one."

Mia Hamm
U.S. Olympic Soccer Player

September 17

"You have to expect things of yourself before you can do them."

Michael Jordan
NBA Player

September 18

"There's no substitute for hard work. If you work hard and prepare yourself, you might get beat, but you'll never lose."

Nancy Lieberman
WNBA Head Coach

September 19

"You should never be proud of doing the right thing. You should just do it."

Dean Smith
College Basketball Head Coach

September 20

"I'd rather regret the risks that didn't work out than the chances I didn't take at all."

Simone Biles
U.S. Olympic Gymnast

September 21

"Today, you have 100% of your life left."

Tom Landry
NFL Head Coach

"You have to remember that the hard days are what make you stronger. The bad days make you realize what a good day is. If you never had any bad days, you would never have that sense of accomplishment!"

Aly Raisman
U.S. Olympic Gymnast

September 23

"Today I will do what others won't, so tomorrow I can accomplish what others can't."

Jerry Rice
NFL Player

September 24

"You can't get much done in life if you only
work on the days when you feel good."

Jerry West
NBA Player

September 25

"Passion is a huge prerequisite to winning it makes you willing to jump through hoops, go through all the ups and downs and everything in between to reach your goal."

Kerri Walsh
U.S. Olympic Beach Volleyball Players

September 26

"There is always going to be a reason why you can't do something; your job is to constantly look for the reasons why you can achieve your dreams."

Shannon Miller
U.S. Olympic Gymnast

September 27

"When you fail, you learn a lot about yourself and come back stronger. Life need not have limits. Having an opportunity in life is important but what defines you is what you do with that opportunity."

Richard Whitehead
Paralympian Marathon Runner

September 28

"Never underestimate the power of dreams and the influence of the human spirit. We are all the same in this notion: The potential for greatness lives within each of us."

Wilma Rudolph
U.S. Olympic Runner

September 29

"Once you learn to quit, it becomes a habit."

Vince Lombardi
NFL Head Coach

September 30

If you want it, you've got to give it.

Lenny Wilkens
NBA Player

October

October 1

"If what you did yesterday seems big, you haven't done anything today."

Lou Holtz
College Football Head Coach

October 2

"It's what you learn, after you know it all, that counts."

John Wooden
College Basketball Head Coach

October 3

"Excuses are the tools of the incompetent."

Mike Tomlin
NFL Head Coach

October 4

"I am building a fire, and every day I train, I add more fuel. At just the right moment, I light the match."

Mia Hamm
U.S. Olympic Soccer Player

October 5

"Try not to do too many things at once. Know what you want, the number one thing today and tomorrow. Persevere and get it done."

George Allen
Head NFL Coach

October 6

"If you want to achieve something in life, you have to take risks."

Dipa Karmakar
Indian Olympic Gymnast

October 7

"Success in life comes to those who simply refuse to give up; individuals with vision so strong that obstacles, failure and loss only act as teachings."

Silken Laumann
Canadian Olympic Rower

October 8

"Winning is not a sometime thing; it's an all time thing. You don't win once in a while, you don't do things right once in a while, you do them right all the time. Winning is habit. Unfortunately, so is losing."

Vince Lombardi
NFL Head Coach

October 9

"In the end, the game comes down to one thing: man against man. May the best man win."

Sam Huff
NFL Player

October 10

"The difference between the impossible and the possible lies in a man's determination."

Tommy Lasorda
MLB Manager

October 11

"A champion is someone who does not settle for that day's practice, that day's competition, that day's performance. They are always striving to be better. They don't live in the past."

Briana Scurry
U.S. Olympic Soccer Player

October 12

"Winning isn't everything, but it beats anything that comes in second."

Paul "Bear" Bryant
College Football Coach

October 13

"Just be patient. Let the game come to you. Don't rush. Be quick, but don't hurry."

Earl Monroe
NBA Player

October 14

"Competitive sports are played mainly on a five-and-a-half inch court, the space between your ears."

Bobby Jones
Professional Golfer

"At a young age winning is not the most important thing... the important thing is to develop creative and skilled players with good confidence."

Arsene Wenger
French Football Manager

October 16

"I became a good pitcher when I stopped trying to make them miss the ball and started trying to make them hit it."

Sandy Koufax
MLB Player

October 17

"I don't have to wait for nobody, I move when I wanna move."

Floyd Mayweather
Professional Box

October 18

"Most talented players don't always succeed. Some don't even make the team. It's more what's inside."

Brett Favre
NFL Player

October 19

"Complacency is a continuous struggle that we all have to fight."

Jack Nicklaus
Professional Golfer

October 20

"Be clear in your own mind as to what you stand for. And then stand up for it."

Bill Walsh
NFL Head Coach

October 21

"You fail all the time, but you aren't a failure until you start blaming someone else."

Bum Philips
NFL Head Coach

October 22

"Self-praise is for losers. Be a winner. Stand for something. Always have class, and be humble."

John Madden
NFL Head Coach

October 23

"If you are afraid of confrontation, you are not going to do very well."

Bill Parcels
NFL Head Coach

October 24

"Adversity is an opportunity for heroism."

Marv Levy
NFL Head Coach

"Confidence is a very fragile thing, and it certainly is something that has to start with your mental approach and your ability to respond and stay focused and not allow negative thoughts to enter into your own mind. When you're successful, it's easier to expect success. All of a sudden it's not there, it becomes more of a challenge."

Bill Cowher
NFL Head Coach

October 26

"If you're growing a garden, you need to pull out the weeds, but flowers will die if all you do is pick weeds. They need sunshine and water. People are the same."

Bill Walsh
NFL Head Coach

October 27

"A CHAMPION is simply someone who did NOT give up when they wanted to."

Tom Landry
NFL Head Coach

October 28

"Failures are expected by losers, ignored by winners."

Joe Gibbs
NFL Head Coach

October 29

"My philosophy? Simplicity plus variety."

Hank Stram
NFL Head Coach

October 30

"For me the starting point for everything—
before strategy, tactics, theories, managing,
organizing, philosophy, methodology, talent,
or experience—is work ethic."

Bill Walsh
NFL Head Coach

October 31

"People don't understand that when I grew up, I was never the most talented, I was never the biggest, I was never the fastest, I certainly was never the strongest. The only thing I had was my work ethic, and that's been what has gotten me this far."

Tiger Woods
Professional Golfer

November

November 1

"The ONLY discipline that lasts, is SELF discipline."

Bum Phillips
NFL Head Coach

November 2

"Life is not a spectator sport. If you're going to spend your whole life in the grandstand just watching what goes on, in my opinion you're wasting your life."

Jackie Robinson
MLB Player

November 3

"It is not the honor that you take with you, but the heritage you leave behind."

Branch Rickey
MLB Executive

November 4

"I worry about the things I can affect, and the things I have no control over I move by."

Lenny Wilkens
NBA Head Coach

November 5

Achievement is largely the product of steadily raising one's levels of aspiration and expectation.

Jack Nicklaus
Professional Golfer

November 6

"Simply by making the effort to start
something, you will be miles ahead of almost
everyone else."

Gary Player
Professional Golfer

November 7

"Don't let talent get in way of team performance. Great players do what's outstanding for team, not what makes them stand out."

Jerry West
NBA Player

November 8

"No matter how good you get, you can always get better and thats the exciting part."

Tiger Woods
Professional Golfer

November 9

"Winners act like winners before they're winners . . . The culture precedes positive results. It doesn't get tacked on as an afterthought on your way to the victory stand. Champions behave like champions before they're champions; they have a winning standard of performance before their winners.

Bill Walsh
NFL Head Coach

November 10

"Knowing is not enough, we must apply.
Willing is not enough, we must do."

Bruce Lee
Professional Mixed Martial Artist

November 11

"Remember this. Hold on to this. This is the only perfection there is, the perfection of helping others. This is the only thing we can do that has any lasting meaning. This is why we're here."

Andre Agassi
Professional Tennis Player

November 12

"There is a point in every contest when sitting on the sidelines is not an option."

Dean Smith
College Basketball Head Coach

November 13

"You can see and you can listen, but you have to have moments in which you feel."

Mike Krzyzewski
College Basketball Head Coach

November 14

"The five S's of sports training are: stamina, speed, strength, skill, and spirit; but the greatest of these is spirit."

Ken Doherty
Irish Professional Snooker Player

November 15

Be led by your dreams. Not by your problems.

Roy Williams
College Basketball Head Coach

November 16

"When you're riding, only the race in which you're riding is important."

Bill Shoemaker
Horseracing Jockey

November 17

"It's supposed to be hard. If it wasn't hard, everyone would do it. The hard is what makes it great."

Jimmy Dugan
A League Of Their Own

November 18

"Overpower. Overtake. Overcome."

Serena Williams
Professional Tennis Player

November 19

"You have to do something in your life that is honorable and not cowardly if you are to live in peace with yourself."

Larry Brown
NBA Head Coach

November 20

"I know how to smile, I know how to laugh, I know how to play. But I know how to do these things only after I have fulfilled my mission."

Nadia Comaneci
Romanian Olympic Gymnast

November 21

"Don't be too proud to take lessons. I'm not."

Jack Nicklaus
Professional Golfer

November 22

"When time is running out and the score is close, most players are thinking, I don't want to be the one to lose the game, but I'm thinking, What do I have to do to win?"

Jerry West
NBA Player

November 23

"Success doesn't care which road you take
to get to its doorstep."

Bill Walsh
NFL Head Coach

November 24

"To be an overachiever you have to be an over-believer."

Dabo Swinney
College Football Head Coach

November 25

"Your TALENT determines what you can do. Your MOTIVATION determines how much you are willing to do. Your ATTITUDE determines how well you do it."

Lou Holtz
College Football Head Coach

November 26

"I never left the field saying I could have done more to get ready and that gives me piece of mind."

Peyton Manning
NFL Player

November 27

"You find that you have peace of mind and can enjoy yourself, get more sleep, and rest when you know that it was a one hundred percent effort that you gave—win or lose."

Gordie Howe
NHL Player

November 28

"If you don't want responsibility, don't sit in the big chair. To be successful, you must accept full responsibility."

College Basketball Head Coach

November 29

"I smile at obstacles."

Tiger Woods
Professional Golfer

November 30

"Sports serve society by providing vivid examples of excellence."

George F. Will
Sports Writer

December

December 1

"Don't measure yourself by what you have accomplished, but by what you should have accomplished with your ability."

John Wooden
College Football Head Coach

December 2

"The man with the ball is responsible for what happens to the ball."

Branch Rickey
MLB Executive

December 3

"We should never discourage young people from dreaming dreams."

Lenny Wilkens
NBA Head Coach

December 4

"We create success or failure on the course primarily by our thoughts."

Gary Player
Professional Golfer

December 5

"Anything can happen with hard work and dedication."

Jerry West
NBA Player

December 6

"Confidence is a lot of this game or any game. If you don't think you can, you won't."

Jerry West
NBA Player

December 7

"The ability to help the people around me self-actualize their goals underlines the single aspect of my abilities and the label that I value most—teacher."

Bill Walsh
NFL Head Coach

December 8

"You can't be afraid to play. Commit to play and you live with the results."

Dabo Swinney
College Football Head Coach

December 9

"My motto was always to keep swinging. Whether I was in a slump or feeling badly or having trouble off the field, the only thing to do was keep swinging."

Hank Aaron
MLB Player

December 10

"The best teams have chemistry. They communicate with each other and sacrifice personal glory for the common goal."

Dave DeBusschere
MLB Player

December 11

"Treat a person as he is, and he will remain as he is. Treat him as he could be, and he will become what he should be."

Jimmy Johnson
NFL Head Coach

December 12

"When you've got something to prove, there's
nothing greater than a challenge."

Terry Bradshaw
NFL Player

December 13

"Make sure your worst enemy doesn't live between your own two ears."

Laird Hamilton
Professional Surfer

December 14

"I think sports gave me the first place where this awkward girl could feel comfortable in my own skin. I think that's true for a lot of women—sports gives you a part of your life where you can work at something and you look in the mirror and you like that person."

Teri McKeever
US Olympic Swim Coach

December 15

"What you lack in talent can be made up with desire, hustle, and giving 110 percent at the time."

Don Zimmer
MLB Coach

December 16

"If you train hard, you'll not only be hard,
you'll be hard to beat."

Herschel Walker
NFL Player

December 17

"Your biggest opponent isn't the other guy. It's human nature."

Bobby Knight
College Basketball Head Coach

December 18

"It ain't over till it's over."

Yogi Berra
MLB Player

December 19

"What keeps me going is not winning, but the quest for reaching potential in myself as a coach and my kids as divers. It's the pursuit of excellence."

Ron O'Brien
US Diving Coach

December 20

"The highest compliment that you can pay me is to say that I work hard every day, that I never dog it."

Wayne Gretzky
NHL Player

December 21

"Winning isn't getting ahead of others. It's getting ahead of yourself."

Roger Staubach
NFL Player

December 22

"For EVERY pass I caught in a game, I caught a THOUSAND in practice."

Don Hutson
Green Bay Packers

December 23

"There is always someone better than you. Whatever it is that you do for a living, chances are, you will run into a situation in which you are not as talented as the person next to you. That's when being a competitor can make a difference in your fortunes."

Pat Summit
College Basketball Head Coach

December 24

"When you're GOOD at something, you'll tell everyone. When you're GREAT at something, they'll tell you."

Walter Payton
NFL Player

December 25

"There are no traffic jams along the extra mile."

Roger Staubach
NFL Player

December 26

"Let the light that shines in you be brighter than the light that shines on you."

Dabo Swinney
College Football Head Coach

December 27

"The effectiveness of a leader is best judged by the actions of those he guides."

Bill Courtney
High School Football Coach

December 28

"A lot of leaders fail because they don't have the bravery to touch that nerve or strike that chord."

Kobe Bryant
NBA Player

December 29

"Talent is God given. Be humble. Fame is man-given. Be grateful. Conceit is self-given. Be careful."

John Wooden
College Basketball Head Coach

December 30

"Attack each day with an enthusiasm
unknown to mankind."

Jim Harbaugh
College Football Head Coach

December 31

"Discover your gift, develop your gift, and then give it away every day."

Don Meyer
College Basketball Head Coach